What Miss Mitchell Saw

written by
Hayley Barrett

illustrated by
Diana Sudyka

Beach Lane Books • New York London Toronto Sydney New Delhi

On the first day of August, in a house tucked away on the fog-wrapped island of Nantucket, a baby girl was born.

Like all babies, this baby was given a name. Her parents whispered it to her like a gentle breeze,

ma...Rye...ah...

At first, little Maria knew
only her mother and father,
her older brother and sister,
and the simple rooms of home.

But as she grew, Maria came to know her island. She rambled its gull-dappled dunes. She breathed the fragrance of its wild roses. She listened to the creak of whaleships come to harbor laden with heavy barrels and homesick boys.

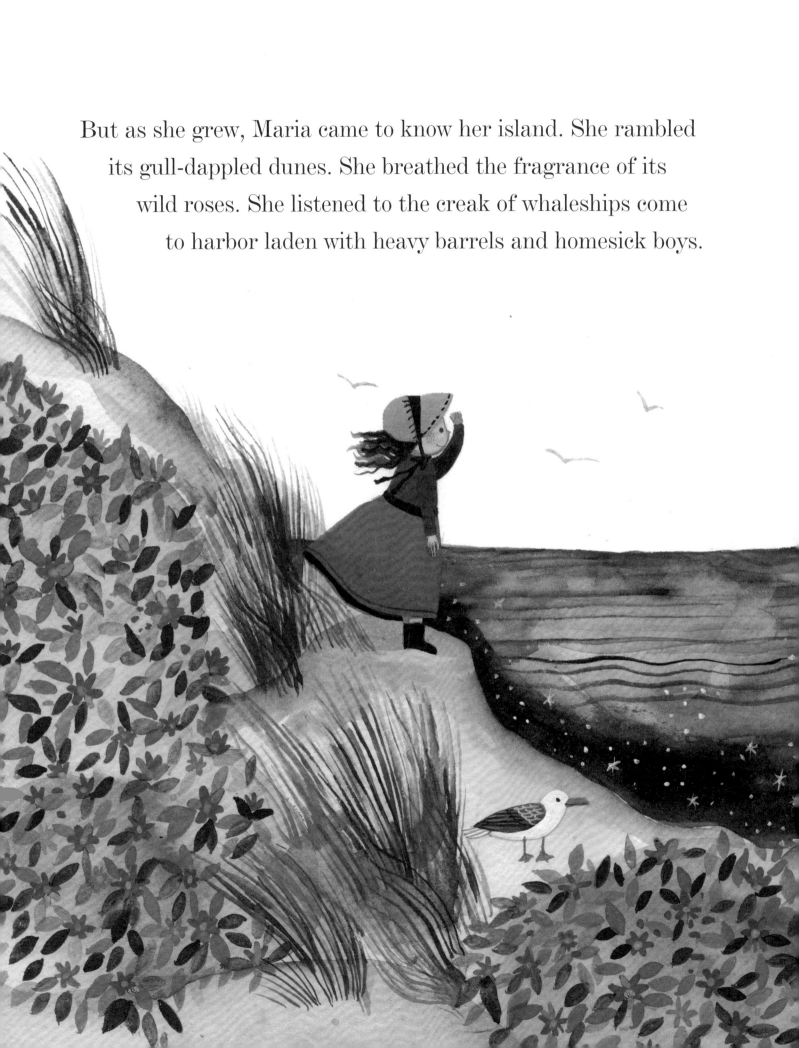

She knew the ships by name.

Maria lived near town and often walked the long
hill of Main Street, down to the crowded wharves and
back up toward the grand brick edifice of the Pacific Bank.
Along the way, she passed the bustle of many shops.

She knew the shopkeepers by name.

POLLY BURNELL BETSEY CARY ELIZA RIDDELL

At home, Maria was trusted with tasks large and small.
Schoolwork did not always come easily, but she studied
with determination.

Mother took note of Maria's steady ways.
When her husband sought someone
to assist him as he observed
the night sky, Mother
said to Maria,

THEE IS the ONE to HELP FATHER.

So Maria and her father climbed up, up, up the steep attic stairs to the walkway on their rooftop, high above Nantucket Town. Together, they gazed at the night sky that cupped their island like a vast, black bowl.

Father taught Maria to use a telescope. He taught her
to sweep the sky carefully—bit by bit—as thoroughly
as she would sweep a room for Mother.
He liked to say,

THEE MUST WONDER.

Maria watched and she wondered. She saw
for herself and was captivated. From then
on, night after night, Maria swept the sky.

She made fast friends with stars that
shone as if punched into the black
with a whalebone needle.

She knew the stars by name.

POLARIS

RIGEL

SPICA

She observed planets that glowed
as steadily as whale oil lamps.

MERCURY

She knew the planets by name.

VENUS

SATURN

She marveled at the celestial phenomena
that arched overhead like a
whale's sparkling splash.

She knew the phenomena by name too.

ECLIPSE

AURORA

Ship captains, home for a while from their whaling, relied on the Mitchells to help them navigate. They brought chronometers—costly timepieces made to withstand ocean voyages—to the little house on Vestal Street.

By her father's side, Maria learned to rate the chronometers. Using a sextant and careful calculation, she determined their accuracy so that sailors at sea might establish their position and, when their arduous work was at an end, set a course toward family and Nantucket Town.

Maria knew the whalers by name.

THE FOLGERS

HER OWN BROTHER ANDREW

THE STARBUCKS

For a while, Maria was a teacher.

But she intended to advance her own education too.

So she became a librarian. Her quiet hours at
the Atheneum were devoted to the study of
advanced mathematics and celestial navigation.

And year after year, when day was done and darkness
settled over Nantucket, Maria climbed the steep stairs
to her rooftop to sweep the sky.

One clear October evening, Maria saw something new:
a nameless patch of light, bright and blurry,
not far from familiar Polaris.

A comet!

She hurried to tell her father.

"My Maria," he exclaimed,

THEE MUST TELL the WORLD

The letter, bound
for Boston, took two
long days to leave
stormy Nantucket.

Half a world away, other stargazers scoured the skies. The king of Denmark had pledged a gold medal to any astronomer who discovered a new comet with a telescope.

FREDERICK the SIXTH

Finding one of these hurtling chunks of ice and gas was a rare feat, and many hoped to win gold and glory.

In a grand observatory in Rome, an astronomer-priest spotted the same bright bit of light. He immediately sent word to claim the medal.

But Maria had seen
the comet first!

The letter from Nantucket,
dated two days before the priest's
sighting, slowly made its way
across the ocean.

It passed, hand to hand, from the
astronomers of Harvard College
to the astronomers of England,
to the astronomers
of Denmark.

HARVARD COLLEGE
OBSERVATORY

Maria knew the Harvard astronomers by name.
They were family friends.

She had not met the others but knew them by name as well.

While these men of science considered the dilemma
of who ought to rightfully claim the medal,
Maria swept the sky.

While they scrutinized the
letter from Nantucket,
Maria swept the sky.

While they consulted the
astronomer-priest of Rome,
Maria swept the sky.

At long last, they concurred and affirmed Miss Mitchell's discovery.

And so the heavy gold medal made its way across the ocean to Boston, to Nantucket, and to Maria's steady hand.

The King of Denmark sent it with his compliments.

The medal was inscribed with the name her parents gave her,
the name known
to shopkeepers,
to sea captains,
to sailors,
and to schoolchildren—
Maria Mitchell.

And it bore the motto:

NOT IN VAIN
the SETTING

DO WE WATCH
and the RISING
of the STARS.

Miss Mitchell saw a comet.

The world saw her.

"The more we see, the more we are capable of seeing." — *Maria Mitchell*

A Bit More about Maria Mitchell—Astronomer, Educator, Activist

★ The comet twenty-nine-year-old Maria Mitchell found at 10:30 p.m. on October 1, 1847, is still known as "Miss Mitchell's Comet."

✳ Father Francesco de Vico, head astronomer of the Vatican observatory, identified the same comet on October 3, 1847. Three other astronomers spotted the comet around the same time, but the scientific community agreed that Maria Mitchell saw it first.

✳ Miss Mitchell's Comet—official astronomical name C/1847 T1—is a nonperiodic comet, which means the shape of its orbit indicates that it will never return to our solar system.

★ Some comets can be seen with the naked eye, but many more can be located and observed with the help of telescopes. A "telescopic comet," one otherwise too faint and far away to be seen, can thus be observed and documented, helping to advance cometary science.

✳ Maria Mitchell was the first American astronomer to win the Danish medal, but she was not the first woman to discover a telescopic comet. German astronomer Caroline Herschel possesses that distinction.

✳ Maria cared little for the international fame that accompanied her discovery. She attended to her work and kept the gold medal in her room.

✳ Maria went on to a distinguished career. Here are some highlights:
  - She was the first woman astronomer employed by the United States government. Beginning in 1849, she computed astronomical tables for the planet Venus for the Nautical Almanac Office. She also made observations for the Coast Survey.

  - She was the first professor hired at the newly founded Vassar Female College, now Vassar College, and she spent nearly the rest of her life teaching astronomy there. Many of her students went on to have notable careers, including Mary Watson Whitney, who became director of the Vassar Observatory after Professor Mitchell's retirement.

  - Maria Mitchell was a staunch advocate for equal pay and disputed with Vassar's administration about salary inequities between female and male professors.

  - She was the first woman elected to the American Academy of Arts and Sciences.

  - Maria Mitchell cofounded the Association for the Advancement of Women. She acted as its president from 1874 until 1876.

- Maria Mitchell was inducted into the National Women's Hall of Fame in 1994.

- She was active in efforts to further women's rights, especially the right to vote, and was a lifelong champion of education for women. She was also active in the anti-slavery movement.

- Like many nineteenth-century Nantucketers, the Mitchells were Quakers, members of the Religious Society of Friends. The Quaker values Maria Mitchell learned at home and in her community—independent thought, diligence, equality of education for girls and boys, and universal human dignity—prepared her to both pursue a remarkable career and to advocate for the rights of others. At that time, some Quakers adopted a "plain" style of speech to reflect their belief in the equality of all people. They avoided the use of titles and addressed others by name or as "thee" and "thou." Although Maria Mitchell eventually left the Society of Friends, she employed plain speech, especially with family members, for the rest of her life. Contemporary Quakers continue to affirm the same values.

- Maria did not have children of her own, but she was a devoted aunt to her nieces and nephews and a trusted friend to many young people. One of Miss Mitchell's Vassar students named her daughter Maria Mitchell Champney, in admiration of her professor and friend.

- The Mitchell crater on the moon is named for her, as is Asteroid 1455 Mitchella.

- Maria Mitchell died on June 28, 1889, at the age of 70. She is buried near where she was born, under the vast black bowl of stars on her quiet island of Nantucket.

A Note from the Author

I live in Massachusetts, so I've been able to visit Nantucket, Maria Mitchell's island birthplace. Wild roses still scent the breeze, the dunes are still dappled with gulls, and, thanks to curator Jascin Leonardo Finger, the Mitchell House on Vestal Street still feels like a happy home.

The house is a museum now, part of the Maria Mitchell Association. Visitors can peek into the bedroom where Maria was born and peer up at the roof walk where she helped her father sweep the skies. Every August 1, in celebration of Maria Mitchell's birthday, her royal medal is put on display there for all to admire.

I wish I could remember when I first heard of Maria Mitchell. I expect I read about her as a child, and she stayed with me. Many of my ideas come this way, from snippets of information I read or heard somewhere. They tug at my imagination, maybe for years, until I begin to write.

I encourage you to pay attention to interesting snippets of information. Collect them. Write them down. Let them tug at your imagination. Watch, wonder, and, like Maria Mitchell, become captivated. Then you will see for yourself.

For a bibliography and suggested further reading about Maria Mitchell,
visit HayleyBarrett.com.

For John,
my steadfast and shining star—H. B.

For Mom, Isa,
and the Pleiades—D. S.

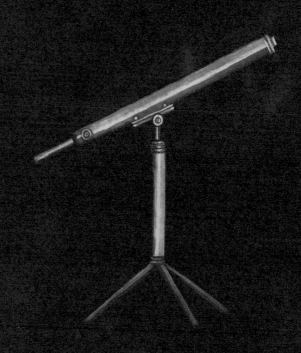

BEACH LANE BOOKS • An imprint of Simon & Schuster Children's Publishing Division • 1230 Avenue of the Americas, New York, New York 10020 • Text copyright © 2019 by Hayley Barrett • Illustrations copyright © 2019 by Diana Sudyka • All rights reserved, including the right of reproduction in whole or in part in any form. • BEACH LANE BOOKS is a trademark of Simon & Schuster, Inc. • For information about special discounts for bulk purchases, please contact Simon & Schuster Special Sales at 1-866-506-1949 or business@simonandschuster.com. • The Simon & Schuster Speakers Bureau can bring authors to your live event. For more information or to book an event, contact the Simon & Schuster Speakers Bureau at 1-866-248-3049 or visit our website at www.simonspeakers.com. • Book design by Lauren Rille • The text for this book was set in De Vinne. • The illustrations for this book were rendered in gouache watercolor and ink. • Manufactured in China • 1021 SCP • 10 9 8 7 6 5 4 3 • Library of Congress Cataloging-in-Publication Data • Names: Barrett, Hayley, author. | Sudyka, Diana, illustrator. • Title: What Miss Mitchell saw / Hayley Barrett ; illustrated by Diana Sudyka. • Description: First edition. | New York : Beach Lane Books, [2019] | Audience: Ages 4–8. | Audience: K to grade 3. | Includes bibliographical references and index. • Identifiers: LCCN 2019000751 | ISBN 9781481487597 (hardcover : alk. paper) | ISBN 9781481487603 (eBook) • Subjects: LCSH: Mitchell, Maria, 1818-1889—Juvenile literature. | Women astronomers—United States—Biography. | Astronomers—United States—Biography. | Comets—Juvenile literature. • Classification: LCC QB36.M7 B37 2019 | DDC 520.92 [B] —dc23 LC record available at https://lccn.loc.gov/2019000751